Coloring Books For Adults Vol. 6

40 Stress Relieving And Relaxing Patterns

Adult Coloring Books Series By
www.ColoringCraze.com

ISBN: 1521172315
ISBN-13: 978-1521172315
Edition: 4

FREE GIFT FOR YOU!

Coloring books enthusiast? Get **Free Bonus Kit** from the site below:

=> http://www.coloringcraze.com/**bonus** <=

Test Your Colors Here

Blend Colors Here

MIX   MIX   MIX

MIX   MIX   MIX

MIX   MIX   MIX

Test Your Colors Here

Blend Colors Here

MIX   MIX   MIX

MIX   MIX   MIX

MIX   MIX   MIX

FROM THE AUTHOR

Thanks for coloring our book! I hope it was relaxing and I hope you had a lot of fun with it.

I would like to ask you for a *small* favor. Book reviews are very important for other coloring enthusiasts like you.

If you have a minute, please leave a comment under our book here: www.coloringcraze.com/**review6**

It will help the buyers to make a decision and your feedback will be priceless to our illustrators ☺

All our other books are available here: www.coloringcraze.com/**our-books**

Remember to grab your **Free Bonus!**

=> http://www.coloringcraze.com/**bonus** <=

Thank You!